When Mommy Feels Sad

A Mother's Journey Through Depression

*Dear Liz —
Thank you for your
support!
Heidi Bartle*

Heidi Bartle

Illustrated by Nathan Allred

ISBN 978-1-63885-978-9 (Paperback)
ISBN 978-1-63885-979-6 (Digital)

Covenant Books
11661 Hwy 707
Murrells Inlet, SC 29576
www.covenantbooks.com

When Mommy Feels Sad is a MUST READ! Finally, a book that offers clear and simple ways for children to understand what depression is and how it can impact family relationships. Heidi Bartle offers understanding, hope, and a safe place for kids to begin asking questions about depression. There is no other children's book on depression like it!

—Barbara Murray, LCSW, Author of *Taking Back Parenting*

Depression is real! Depression is hard! It hurts individuals *and* families. Heidi has found a way to help children understand what depression really is, how it affects others, and how to get hope. Every home should have this book to help kids understand depression too!

—Jim R. Jacobs, LCSW, Author of *Driving Lessons For Life: Thoughts on Navigating Your Road to Personal Growth*

To those who suffer and those who care for the suffering:
May you find hope in your journey.

In a beautiful city near the mountains sat a cozy little house.
It was a lovely place surrounded by trees and flowers, and inside lived a
happy family.

The mother loved her husband and children more than anything.
They laughed and played in the park, read stories together, and drew chalk people
in the driveway.

Sometimes there were arguments and messes in the happy little house, but the mother and father and the children worked together to make things right.

The mother had every reason to be happy.
She lived in a wonderful place. She had the best family and many friends.
She had a beautiful home and a very comfortable life.

But sometimes the mother wasn't happy.

Actually, she felt sad a lot of the time. This was hard for people to understand.
Why would someone with so many reasons to be happy feel sad?

It was an illness.
Some people have trouble with their hearts or their legs or their eyes.
This mother's illness was in her mind. It was called depression.
Depression felt dark and unhappy. She was tired and lonely and very, very sad.

She cried a lot.
She didn't like doing many of the things that had always made her happy, like going to fun places, being outside, and spending time with people.

Even though she loved her family, she often needed to be alone because she felt so sad.
She wanted to get better, and people who loved her wanted to help.
Her family and friends were glad when she met with doctors and took medicine and talked to people who understood what was happening.

Sometimes those things helped her feel better!
The mother could do big, exciting things, like go to a museum or play in the creek or hike up a mountain.
On some days she could go shopping and clean the house and make dinner all in one day.

But some days she stayed in bed and cried.
She didn't know why it happened or how to stop it or, most importantly, how to make it go away.
Doctors wondered: Did something upsetting start the depression? Was her brain causing the problem? Was she just made this way?
The doctors didn't know why her depression started, and they didn't know how to cure it.

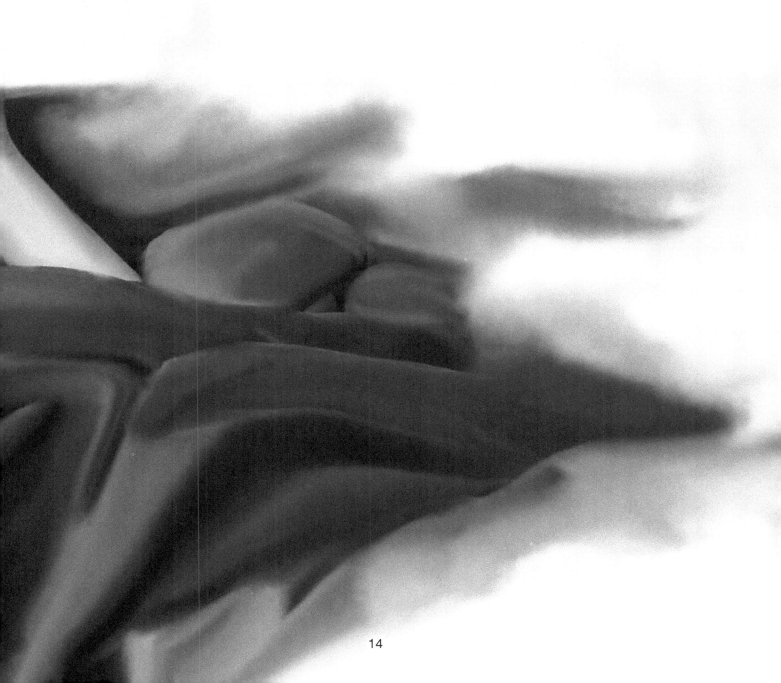

When the mother was upset about her depression, she had many strong feelings.

She felt frustrated.

Why is this happening again?

She felt guilty.

I should be doing more for my family.

She felt disappointed.
Why can't I control this?

She felt embarrassed.

I'm the only one.

She felt ashamed.
I'm not a person. I'm a disease.

She felt worthless.
Only a loser acts this way.

She felt angry.
I hate feeling like this!

She felt hopeless.
Will this ever change?

The mother often hid her feelings. She worried that sharing her sorrow would make people love her less.

She especially didn't want to tell her children when she was feeling depressed. Would *they* love her less?

She knew her illness was hard on her family. They were sad that she was sad. They missed playing with her and doing fun things together. They worried she would be sick for a long time.

She didn't want to be the mom who cries a lot.
She didn't want to stay in bed.
She didn't want to be the impatient mom, the boring mom, the tired mom, the sick mom, the mom who stays home because she is too sad to have fun.

The mother made a list of things that could cheer her up or at least help her get out of bed—especially for her children:

- write in a journal
- take a walk
- read a book
- listen to music
- call a friend
- get outside
- play the piano
- work in the garden
- take a shower
- clean the house
- help someone else

Well…sometimes those things didn't work.

One thing that *did* work almost every time was being with someone who would wipe away her tears and listen to her thoughts and not judge them or her.

Feeling love from people helped the most.

It took a long time (many years) for the mother to accept that she had
an illness, and the depression wasn't her fault.
It was just like asthma or allergies.
She had to see her doctor and take her medicine every day, and even
then, bad days could happen anytime.
But it was okay.

It was okay to have the illness. It was okay to talk about it. It was okay to be unhappy about it. It was okay to cry a lot. It was okay to ask for help.

Most of all, the mother was okay.
Her illness did not define her. She had an illness called depression. She was not depression.
She was valuable and worthy of love and contributed to her family and her community in meaningful ways.

Her family loved her. Her friends loved her.
She didn't have to be alone with her depression. When she needed someone, she could call a family member or a therapist or a friend.
She knew how to ask for help.

I am the mother.
I have depression, and I am often sad.
But I have hope.
I hope for health and healing. I hope for smiles and sunshine. I hope for strength and courage…

even when I can't get out of bed.

Dear Reader,

Before I wrote this book, I was afraid to tell people about my depression. I worried they would think I was making it up or just too lazy to get out of bed. A wonderful person helped me see that sharing would help me heal. I wrote this story to help me talk to my children about my depression. Even before the story had pictures, it became a meaningful way to start conversations about my experience with depression and the difficult feelings that accompanied it. It helped others on their journey toward healing too.

I invite you to share this book and start your own conversations about mental illness. What are your questions? How do you feel? What can you share?

Best wishes for your mental health,
Heidi

Glossary

angry: A strong, uncomfortable feeling of displeasure that something is wrong.

ashamed: A painful feeling that you are a bad person.

cure: A treatment that makes a sick person well.

depression: An illness that makes a person feel unhappy and changes the way they think and act.

disappointed: Feeling sad that something you wanted didn't happen or something happened that you didn't want.

doctor: Someone who has special knowledge about the body and works to help people who are sick. Sometimes a doctor who helps people with depression is called a psychiatrist (si-kahy-uh-trist).

embarrassed: Feeling like something you did or something that happened to you shouldn't have happened and worrying about what others think.

frustrated: Feeling upset that a problem happens again and again.

guilty: Feeling that you haven't done enough or that you have done something wrong.

"Her illness did not define her" (p.33): The thing that makes a person sick (in this story, depression) is not the only thing about him or her. Other parts of that person are good and important too.

hopeless: Feeling that a problem can never be fixed.

illness: Poor health or sickness.

judge: When a person decides how to feel about something, even though he or she might not know everything about it.

medicine: Something a person takes into his or her body, like pills, for example, that helps that person get better. Medicine usually comes from doctors (see above) and should be used carefully.

worthless: Feeling that you are not good enough.

Parent and Teacher Resources

When Mommy Feels Sad can be an important guide in teaching about depression. Parents, teachers, and family members can utilize and expand upon the resources below to have spontaneous or planned conversations that support, instruct, and empower those whose lives are touched by depression.

Discussion Questions

For parents with depression and their children:

- How does it feel to see the mother in the book crying or in bed all the time?
- Do you feel that way when you see me in bed?
- Review pages with strong feelings. Do you have any of these feelings? Do you have other feelings?
- Stress that your depression is not their fault (or yours) and talk about ways your family members can support one another during difficult times.
- Tell the children about the things you are doing to get better. Explain that even though you have depression, you love your children very much.

For students and family members:

- Do you know anyone who is sick with a physical disease? What about a mental illness? How are they different? How are they the same?
- How does the book show the mother trying to take care of herself when she is depressed?
- What could you do to help someone with depression? (Help students/children focus on helping the person with things he or she struggles to do right now, like washing dishes or helping with homework, in addition to helping the person receive proper medical care.)
- What could you say to a friend who tells you that he or she is depressed?

Activities

Grades 3–5:

Reread the section focusing on the strong feelings the mother had when she was depressed. Divide into groups, giving each group one or two emotions to discuss. Have students explain how those emotions feel to them, role-playing how each emotion looks and feels. Ask students to share with the whole class what they learned about their assigned emotions and how they relate to depression.

Writing prompts:

- Write about a time when you felt embarrassed (or another emotion). Why did you feel that way? How did it feel? Did something or someone help you feel better?
- Is the color of each emotion in the book the color you would choose? Why?

See the section below for ideas to teach empathy for those with mental illness. For lesson plans related to depression, visit https://classroom.kidshealth.org/classroom/.

Grades 6–12:

For thorough information about mental illness and suicide prevention, visit https://nimh.nih.gov.

Make a poster or flyer that displays the symptoms of depression. Hang posters and pass out flyers at school to raise awareness of the signs of depression that students can recognize in their friends.

To teach empathy, develop simple scenarios and ask students how they could relate and act. Scenarios might be as follows:

- A friend looks sad but wants to be alone. What might that person be feeling? What could you do or say to help?
- Someone you know takes medicine and sees a therapist for an illness you don't understand. What might that person be feeling? How could you be a supportive friend?

About the Author

Heidi's relationships and activities are colored by bipolar disorder. She is constantly learning how to manage symptoms and appreciate stability. Through the challenge of accepting and embracing her illness, she has learned to advocate for mental health issues and support others in their personal struggles.

Heidi graduated from Brigham Young University, where she studied and worked in the health science field. She and her husband, Garry, run a nonprofit organization called For the Love that supports foster children and underprivileged families in their city. They have five children.

CPSIA information can be obtained
at www.ICGtesting.com
Printed in the USA
JSHW010746230322
24151JS00004B/47